ONE HUNDRED ETUDES

ONE HUNDRED ETUDES

Benjamin Friedlander

Edge Books

ISBN: 978-1-890311-34-6

Edge Books are published by Rod Smith, editor of
Aerial magazine, and distributed by:

Small Press Distribution   Edge Books
1341 Seventh Street   P.O. Box 25642
Berkeley, CA 94710-1409   Georgetown Station
1.800.869.7553   Washington, DC 20027
www.spdbooks.org   aerialedge@gmail.com
orders@spdbooks.org   www.aerialedge.com

ONE HUNDRED ETUDES

En hommage à

Louis Zukofsky. *"Intellect /*

Resigned to / less

Is / susceptible at /

Least to / the

Range / of two /

Sides of / a

Coin"— "A"-19.

For Carla Billitteri

Like rings fitted
Into crushed velvet,

These words—bejeweled,
Inscribed with sentiments
Or tarnished—mere

Ornaments of sense
That would engage
Your willing thought.

One: THE GHOST
OF A CHANCE
For Larry Eigner

To obey what
Might have been
An either/or

Condition of employment
For metaphor takes
Neither intellect, nor

Resignation, but a

Lifetime of labor.

The mind is

A feeble light

Fed by the

Same wind that

Blows it out.

Two: FORT DA

A storm three

Hundred miles away
Interrupts the melody
Of two intersecting

Signals: two birds
Delimiting the sky
Atop the sun-

Crushed peaks of
Snow; the dead
Air swallowing up

Their voices reaching
From below. Stunned
By forms of

Linear constraint. Submerged
In elemental reasoning.
The radio station

Marks us out
Of range. **Three:**
LIBRETTO *for Nick*

Lawrence Deleuze observes

That all great

Events are torn

In two like

Opera tickets. One

Half's added up

With the receipts,

The other's a

Souvenir we get

To keep. In
Vietnam, when Tet
Was staged in

T.V. simulcast,
The troop itself
Was cost and

Keepsake. A quarter
Century later only
Stubs of men

Remain to tell

The younger viewers

Not to trust

Their eyes, but

Listen, listen, listen.

Four: AVANT GARDE

It plunks like

A quarter in

A wishing well,

That isn't a
Well, but a
Still fountain in

A busy museum,
Where change collects
A penny for

Your thoughts. **Five:**
ABANDON Something flew
The cooped up

Feeling of being

In the wrong

For so long

My wings atrophied.

Incredible to merely

Breathe again, what

I could once

Even float upon.

Six: JUDICIAL INTERPRETATION

Wording is nine-
Tenths of the
Law, but those

Who take it
Into their heads
To sweeten the

Pot by betting
On syntax win
It all back

In the sentence.

Seven: THE MIND
IS A BUBBLE

SHEET A thought
Balloon or soap
Bubble. Indistinct picture,

It reveals nothing
But our own
Confusion. Squinting, seeing,

The mindful man
Or woman finds
A penny (heads)

And picks it
Up. Thus chance
Gives necessity body:

A burning pain,
A flickering memory,
A hobbled step

To the door,
Which is locked.
Bewildered or stunned

Silence, it falls
Asleep, wakes again.
Crashes, is restored.

An answering machine
That cuts off
The crucial word,

The mind, hearing
A distant sound,
Becomes a joint

Controlling movement. Tight
Like a smile
Freely dispensed with

Liquor, the mind,
A decimal point
That magnifies experience,

A liquid controlled
By knowable laws.
It has capacity

And gives it:
Like salt dissolved
In water its

Forgotten thought can
Still give taste.
Denture, spectacle, phantom

Pain, it supplies
The body with
What it needs,

Or doesn't need
But stupidly wants:
An automatic rehearsal

Of things going
Round and round.
A mute ant

Lifting a leaf,
The leaf itself:
A captured flag

Gained for pride
But held without
Respect. **Eight:** ROUTE

Memory's branches will
Eventually be stripped.
What grows back

Can never be
The same. But
If we keep

Driving south we'll
See less decay,
More green: more

Money. The vanquished
Who made blood
Shed its connotation

Of defeat, paying
Homage to service
With stemmed-glass

Worship. Their hours
Clop on, driven
By whips. Trampling

Out the neglect
Of a road
To ruined places.

Nine: A MARTIAN
ODE Tortured thoughts
Taking wing in

Hand tear free
From logical sequence:
A systematic derangement

Of the census,
Effected by laughter
In the eye

Of the behemoth.
A widening eye
Blinded by spectacle.

A red eye
Coagulating the sky.
Pull your tongue

Out to examine
Its intention; speak
Softly, capricious god:

Let your voice
Carry its heavy
Mortar far away.

Ten: PATRIOT DAYS
Under a siege
Mentality we know

What we know
Without knowing it
Is not knowledge

We can use.
In the holes
Of a punch

Card, the idea
Of order: properties
Managed, commingled funds.

Troubled by sleep,
Punished by light.
Hard cases locked

From inside. Shoveled

Under a mountain

Of brick, sickened

By lies, by

Sighs tapped out

On prison walls.

Where a razor

Disdains our stubble

To pick through

Rubble, a cramped
Foot gains leverage
Against the sky,

And roving bands
Of barbers sigh
To see another

Statue stumble. **Eleven:**
THE MONUMENT Dullness
And vanity, diving

Like a gull

Into a sea,

Into an argument

With architectural history,

Feed with unabashed

Hunger on a

Sinking scrap of

Knowledge. **Twelve:** AFTER

DIFFICULTY SLEEPING Like

The broken peel
Of a clementine,
Your finished thought

Will not lie
Flat. A rat
Knows. It goes

Every which way
Your mind goes,
Disappearing in holes

No wider than

A sigh, gnawing

What fancy sets

By. **Thirteen:** READYMADE

NOTATION *for Molly*

Nesbit A history

Of brand names

And their generic

Substitutes, which are

Cheaper than the
Original items, but
Just as effective—

Except in art.
Fourteen: DIALECTICAL MATERIALISM
Where to be

Is to be
A corner where
A mop leans,

Its work undone,

Three intersecting plains

Must have come

To some conclusion.

Fifteen: JUNK Why

Is the midnight

Rain so much

More soothing than

A dripping sink?

Though downward stains

Of rust are

How we think

To cling to

Life sometimes. Oxidized

By pleasure we're

Metallic to the

Bone—easily bent,

Or stretched thin

As wire, conducting
Heat by breath
Alone. The torture

Is exquisite when
You're sliding down
The drain, numbed

By a heart's
Measure, and a
Fortune in your

Veins. **Sixteen:** IN
A STATION OF
THE METRO Faces

In a crowd,
Heavy with light.
Their saturated colors

Thicken, weigh reality
Down. **Seventeen:** CUBICLE
Fill each box

With a day
Of life, just
The one life

Every last day.
Eighteen: LEGAL REMEDY
Like a box

Assembled from its
Own contents, this
Pleading: distress signal,

Meter reading, model
Of consciousness deployed
Like a medicine

Chest. A prayer
For relief awaiting
Dismissal. Numbered lines

Filling with keystrokes
A record of
Billable hours. **Nineteen:**

THE SOCIAL BODY

For Elaine Scarry

The carved compassion

Of an upraised
Hand, palm out,
Threaded with flowers,

Breaks off contact
With the future
When it shatters.

Let the absolute
Dissolve in ambiguity,
Sun fall, shadows

Slip away. Let
The fountain scatter
And regather its

Notes in perpetuity—
Divinity has no
Voice: if it

Speaks, you can't
Hear; if you
Listen, it won't

Speak. Transparent, poisonous,
Dispensable air woven
From cloudy thought

Makes the tears
Fall cold, hard,
In a light-

Probed darkness: war

Is a surface

Where the tires

Get a grip

But language can't

Pierce the frozen

Pond where skulls

Are gnawed by

Sealed-off memories

Of peace. **Twenty:**
EDEN I *contain*
A soul? Like

A snail driven
By a shell,
It's dragged along

My slimy track
Helplessly, the garden
A distant memory.

Twenty-one: MATERIALISM

The broken spine

On a book

You can't rebind,

Where the margins

Are too narrow

To begin with,

And your notes

Go right to

The edge. **Twenty-Two:** AMERICA, A PROPHECY *for Alice*

Notley The shotgun
Marriage of heaven
And hell hath

No fury like
A thankless child.
The amniotic fluid

Of a state
Funeral, bearing false
Witness without an

Epidural. **Twenty-three:**
INDULGING THE MOMENT
A pinkish blur

In a steamed
Mirror, after Bonnard:
The corpulent self

Dries off, has
Thoughts, gives ground
To abstract reasoning.

It drops out
Of the plan,
And drags off

The end, into
Beginningless vagaries, overtaken
By crude sensation,

Color and perfume.
Twenty-four: SPRING
Streaks of glass

In asphalt catch
The light and
Turn to water.

In March, the
Hard, bumpy lawns
Support miles of

Sky: the green

Protruding from brown

Pulp's ongoing struggle

With form. Jostled

By highbeams, sunk

Into thought. In

April, the rain

Has a plush

Bottom. **Twenty-five:**

MONEY *for Ezra*
Pound The embalmed
Face of our

Founding father, sounding
The depths of
His grass-colored

Grave, forever alarmed
That his farewell
Address is reduced

To a "keep

The change." **Twenty-**

Six: OUT OF

JURISDICTION *for Ron*

Silliman **A** green

Light turns red

Without regard for

The needs of

Any particular driver,

But by a

Design that would

Serve the needs

Of every driver.

Bathed in light,

A dark continent

Set adrift by

Economic policy sinks

Us: a beach

Bored by the
Sea washing away
Its claim to

The sun. Cities
Like poems, articulate
A syntax derived

From general conditions,
But always adapted
To specific needs—

Or not always,
But always when
Push comes to

Shove. **D**ecrepit balcony,
Precariously raised above
An unsafe street,

Protruding story blocking
The sun, telling
Sign of neglect,

Weather-beaten and
Diminished in value
Like its owner.

Every last erection
Of identity, formed
By a trace

Of irony, supports
Our emotional response
To those who

Demonstrate a capacity

For upending order

With pleasure. **F**ormal

Innovation is nothing

More than an

Extension of suspicious

Contents under pressure—

And this idea,

Extended into social

Planning, explodes in

A summer of

Riots. Grim faced

Young men with

Their eyes on

The prize play

Video games all

Night, their soft

Sloping shoulders easily

Assuming the posture
Of benign neglect.
Human nature: a

System of applied
Knowledge in which
The kinks are

Worked out by
Turning control over
To another system

No better than
The first. Illuminating
The moment, action

Is a darkening
Thought, a light-
Sensitive grimace recalling

An entire scene
To mind: slowing
Cars, flashing lights,

Broken glass, covered
Bodies. Just seen
This morning: an

Orange cat, bones
Crushed, along the
Road, the finality

Of its preciousness
Coalescing in color
Whipping past me

As I drive.

Kaleidoscope of screens

In department-store

Showroom breaking news

Into fundamental facts,

A prism's coalition

Of bent rays

Coloring our view

Of our commander

In chief. **L**et
The avenues stretch
Out like lies,

Like a calculator
Whose plus sign
Reinterprets the sum,

Like a ravaged
Mouth showing urban
Decay up close,

Personal. **M**urky water
Wrinkling in discomfort
As the body

Stirs, pain already
Instigating a change
In attitude, dissolving

Lumps of fear
In blood retreating
Beyond defended boundaries.

Night neither falls
Nor rises, but
Continually kneels, obedient

To the sun
Extending a diminished
Brilliance across eight

Minutes of darkness,
Meting out grace,
Warmth, sight. One's

Experience of time

Times out after

Insufficient activity, allowing

Thought to wander

Aimlessly in space,

Unremarked by grieving

Friends duly notified

By the benefactor

Software. Postmodern architecture

Casts a long
Shadow on the
City, constructing paths

For thought through
Unreachable mirrors, promoting
Growth even where

The sun doesn't
Penetrate our reflections.
Quiet night suddenly

Broken by a
Far-off siren
Approaching the shores

Of consciousness, like
A cold fog
Managing a distance

That only now
Becomes dangerous. Reason
Asserts authority, firmly,

Patiently, ineffectually, a
Quiet child admonishing
A Teddy bear,

Intently staring into
His face, her
Own face lit

Up with self-
Possession. Subjectivity effects
The expected outcome

Of a controlled

Experiment in rage:

The twist-off

Cap's broken smile

Making a crack

When I'm thirsting

For a fight.

The clearance at

The drive-by

Window permits remote
Access, loose change,
Encrypted chit-chat:

A global game
Of telephone creating
A virtual tower

Of Babel. Under
The star-starved
Underside of clouds,

Within the glow
Of a fire,
Forever sealed off

From the real
World by newspapers
Covering an unused

Window. Vibration can
Make a building
Dissolve in tears,

Puddling in garbage-
Strewn lots vacant
As a fridge

Attracting a child:
Subjectivity enclosed in
Its destroyed environ.

Written in dust
On a windshield,
A curse for

No one in
Particular, or everyone:
Pattern without sense,

But sensible, going
With the flow
Of information. **X**

Marks the spot
I'm in but
Not the way

twenty-six

Out, melted snow
Knotted in footprints,
Expressing the difference

Between a human
Life and human
History. **Y**esterday is

The lining of
Today, the skin
Of a glove

Worn by the
World, turned inside
Out, but holding

Out the possibility
Of a future.
Zealous pursuit of

Principle is bound
To break free
From principle: a

Game of cat

And mouse played

By a cat

And mouse isn't

A game. **Twenty-**

Seven: A PENNY

FOR YOUR THOUGHTS

What's the difference

Between poetry and

Politics? One can
Be justified, the
Other is just

Chance operation. Call
It in the
Air, American: "E

Pluribus Unum" or
"In God We
Trust"? **Twenty-eight:**

BY THE ROAD
TO THE CONTAGIOUS
HOSPITAL *for Bob*

Perelman Brake lights
Ahead signal delay,
Where the minute

Hand turns like
A child-proof
Cap. Eroding points

Of observation. Curtsying
Buildings, alloyed steel.
Where cars pass,

Apples bruise, skin
Discolors and another
Winter recedes, returns.

Through unknown waves
Of radio, sun
In the miles

twenty-eight

Leading us past
Blown flakes, mist,
A day's legibility,

Rehearsed the day
Before the day
Of reckoning. Accounts

Receivable: the dead
Air swallowing sound.
The mercury dropping

Its guard, smelling
Of corruption, drift.
Mine eyes have

Seen the glory
Mourning a wilted
Flower's disconnection from

The sun. Staggered
By affection, numbed
By dimming light,

Decaying beauty plunges
Into color, liquefies
The dying day.

Where the stress
Of waiting patiently
Might crack a

Tooth if not
Reality, the mind
Is a grooved

Surface on a
Toll road with
Numbered exits. **Twenty-**

Nine: CAPTION FOR
A PHOTOGRAPH *for
David Levi Strauss*

The orphan frown
Of a war-
Torn town, healed

By a clumsy

Caress, stands on

Ceremony, not on

Legs, and speaks,

But under duress.

Thirty: A LITTLE

BOOK *for Robert*

Creeley ANSWERING MACHINE

A slurred question

Brings the memory
Of a face
Right here, while

There, in memory,
Another's intonation lingers.
AN ENLIVENING ANGER

An enlivening, misdirected
Anger, now aimed
Precisely, but without

Joy, at its

Appropriate target. THE

APPROPRIATE TARGET Here,

In a box

Of my own

Fabrication, hammered shut

From the inside.

PHENOMENON The characteristic

Of a thing

Is a thing
With a characteristic:
The fuzzed branch

Tugged by sky,
The spider holding
Sway above my

Bed, are agencies
Of recognition. Put
In the world

Put in my

Head by perception.

ARTIFICE In squiggle

Lies giggle, in

God we trust.

The gender of

A rock shaped

By ancient hands.

INTUITION A tincture

Of ink in
Clear water, changing
The whole, but

Without committing itself
Totally. HURT BIRD
A roving signal,

Grasping at wind.
WAR The situation
Is fluid, whirling

Signs of power
Brought down flicker
In the windows.

LIKE Like a
Simile too clever
By half. DAYDREAM

We leave our
Heads on the
Shelf when we

Close the book.
FRIENDLY ADVICE Jiggle
The key when

You get home
Free. BREATHE ON,
OLD MEAT I've

Spent my life
Splitting hairs, and
Now they're gray.

IN THIS BAR
The president is
Background noise. FAMILY

Mother and father,
Brother and sister,
Me. A five-

Sided, three-dimensional
Object with shifting
Angles, existing primarily

In the mind.
THE MIND Restless,
Seeking stasis. BIRD

Lift your wings
Like a voice,
Or vice versa.

I.C.U.
Face to face
With your mortality,

Reflecting now unthinkingly
Our own. WHITE
CHRISTMAS Drifts and

Piles shoveled into
Order. JOB WELL
DONE i's dotted,

T's crossed. EXCITEMENT
Zigzagging dogs draw
The authorities. PERSONAGE

Thick-waisted thistle
In a yard.
REALITY A prison

Whose walls have
Yet to be
Discovered. THE WEDGE

Where each end-
Stopped thought, breathing,
Hesitates, feeling forms

A sediment. SEDIMENT
Spiritless imagining dirty
Furious ominous disputatious

Leaving tears bitterness
Echoes anger all
Of it fought.

ALL All my
Thought is broken
Stupidly into words.

WORDS Deliberate as

The bus heeding

Every stop. DEAD

BATTERY Time stopped

The clock's advance.

LANGUAGE Mind and

Body joined at

The tongue. NATURE

Golden ants gather

Around a brown
Beetle's crushed armor.
MNEMONIC DEVICE *for*

Jackson Mac Low
My very eccentric
Mother just said

Up now please.
Thirty-one: QUIPS
You can fleece

A lamb at

Market but you

Can't make it

Mink. You can

Lead a clotheshorse

To a watering

Hole, but you

Can't make him

Think. You can

Respect but never
Embrace a man
Who stands aloof.

Reality: an unconvincing
Proposition refusing convincing
Proof. Let twitching

Dogs sleep and
Let bewitching fogs
Creep over us

Like an allusion.
The dogged purpose
Of life is

Not strained, but
Maintained, by canine
Dreams, when all

Is not as
It seems. **Thirty-
Two:** AT GOD'S

TABLE Time crawled

Like an ant

Across the length

Of a sigh,

Only to fall

Into a moment

Shallower than a

Spoon. Lifted from

A bowl deeper

Than hope, stirring

Thoughts of future

Moments, drowned in

Sighs of understanding.

Thirty-three: JEWISH

STUDIES *Creation* Something

New-fangled, tangled

In consciousness: beauty

Of a mind

Plunged into unseen
Light. *Promise* Generation
Is a flood

Filling the days
To come. Beyond
Reach, a rainbow

Gathering all color
Together, holding back
The sky. *Prayer*

Like a boat
Fondled by waves,
The letters pass

Along the swellings
Of a voice—
And stop, straining

Against the anchor
Of the hope.
Prophecy History, driven

From prayer, lets
The private utterance
Declare its public

Aim: the difference
Between what must
Be and is,

Rendered as sound
Run aground. *Diaspora*
What strange bunk

We lie on

In chains, free

To read of

Better days. *Emancipation*

The world is

My harbor, my

Vessel is free

To be lashed

Anywhere cities entice,

Waves call. *Inscription*
Blue blue sea
Passing beyond me,

Dissimulating shores await
Your anchored prayer's
Uncertain fate: *adieu.*

Thirty-four: URBAN
RENEWAL The horn
Is a born

Politician, not for

What he says

(He says nothing),

But for how

He pleads for

Our attention, just

To clear a

Path for our

Removal. **Thirty-five:**

AFTER THE POST-
MODERN Art lies,
Even when it

Tells the truth.
Lies still, embalmed,
Waiting for a

Service. **Thirty-six:**
REFERENDUM Put it
To a vote

Of the people
Of Maine, they
Can stomp their

Dreams like feet
That have fallen
Asleep and now

Tingle with apprehension,
Of more movement
To the right,

Like a dial
Catching nothing but
Static. **Thirty-seven:**

DICTATION The mind
Is a single-
Family dwelling filled

With cheap pre-
Fab furnishings. Then
Something enters from

Outside (call it
The movers, the
Marshalls, the martians)

To repossess your
Junk. The sheet
Rock crumpled like

A first draft,
Shook from thought
Like a drawing

From an etch-
A-sketch. On
The other side

Of the mirror
Image of the
Gesture reaching out

To the tinted
Company debriefing us
Behind glass. *Stiffen,*

Pencil, be known
To the page.
Like the sting

Of a jellyfish,
A dawning idea
Lets the objects

Of memory pierce
Dark thoughts. Beggar,
Your cup drinks

In the view
Of our averted
Eyes. The cliff

Rubs the sea
The wrong way
And comes off

In our hands,
An ugly incident
From sleep fondling

Facts repelling interpretation.

A storage device

Or entombed body,

Quivering gelatin or

Impression of teeth,

The poem, hard

Pressed into paper

Expectant underneath. **Thirty-Eight:** INDEPENDENCE DAY

For Paul Beatty
Our huddled masses
Just can't wait

For the pie-
Hole in the
Sky to operate

The soft ice-
Cream cone machine.
Let freedom bling

Bling, Shaq. Like
A dripping popsicle
Torn in half.

One nation under
God knows what
Thumb, with liberty

Bell souvenirs for
All. **Thirty-nine:**
AFTER RIMBAUD *I*

Is an ant-

Isocial being, a

Colony unto itself,

Kicking up sand

Around its hole

As it digs

Levels of meaning

Intruders will never

Know. **Forty:** SPEECH

ACT *for Michael*

Davidson A spelling

Dictionary balled into

A fist resists

Translation, but incompletely.

The word become

Object of human

Exchange; its silence

Is a golden

Mean. Let sense

Beyond grasp be

Music to other

Ears. Our poems

Command more: lower

Limit gesture, upper

Limit caress. For

We who hear

Our syllables disintegrate

Under stress, still
Hold the power
To communicate with

Reasonable success. **Forty-
One:** THROUGH A
GLASS Divine shapes

Drawn from light—
Like a splinter
From an eye.

They speak, shielding
The glare, their
High heads aloft

In the clouds
In the crowd,
Seeming to see

Furred colors, living
Shapes. The tiniest
Spiders march across

The day; equivocal

Mountains, the clouds,

Mass triumphantly, blow

North. Where feelings

Have a railing

But the stairs

Are gone, I

See the glory

Of a distance

Attended by stars.
Forty-two: STREAMING
AUDIO *for Charles*

Bernstein It makes
No sense: wit
Makes no sense

Sharper, but cuts
Thought to ribbons.
Like typewriter keys

At a cross

Purpose, sounds bunch

Together and communication

Comes to a

Sudden stop. **Forty-**

Three: THE SOCIAL

PRODUCTION OF MEANING

For Norma Cole

Between regret and

Recognition, consciousness blinks
On and off.
A difference in

The dark, a
New moon, cuts
To the quick-

Tempered sickness of
What you want.
The constitution of

The reality of
These wrongs. A
Siren in the

Night sings to
Me somebody else's
Trouble. **Forty-four:**

PUSHING THE ARTFORM
For Kenneth Goldsmith
Wynton Marsalis, the

Most acclaimed jazz
Musician and composer
Of his generation,

As well as
Distinguished classical performer,
Recipient of the

Grand Prix du
Disque of France,
The Edison award—

Netherlands, 23 honorary

Doctorates, and the

1997 Pulitzer Prize

For music: The

First ever for

Jazz. Movado, maker

Of some of

The most acclaimed

Timepieces in history,

Holds 99 patents,
Over 200 international
Awards for design,

And has watches
In museums on
Five continents: A

Leader in innovation.
Forty-five: DREAM-
DEFERRED EARNINGS Crashing

Through bores, REM
Sleep blinks off
Another round of

Target practice. Here
Where wonders never
Seize the means

Of pre-production,
Teams of Siamese
Cats hunt mice

In tandem. Random

Access, your holes

Fill up with

Words, words, words.

Your ruination's a

Rumination of bombed-

Out syllogisms punching

A clock. **Forty-**

Six: X-RATED

T-SHIRT What

Doesn't spill you

Makes you harder.

Forty-seven: DEDICATION

If it's trampled

It's a heart.

If it rises

Up it beats

Your voice into

A grave matter
Of print. Love
Requires no language

But accepts it
In stone. Teeth
Scattered like seeds

Planting a question:
Why? No answer
Comes knocking, only

Men in uniform
Like you, bearing
A flag. **Forty-**

Eight: ENJOY YOUR
SYMPTOM! Bizarro Superman,
Your diamond-facet

Face, white as
Porcelain, proclaims nothing
But the violence

Of history. Universal
Spirit: the insistence
Of the letter

S on your
Fluttering cape escaped
Our notice. **Forty-**

Nine: NOTHING REMAINS
SAVE ALL HISTORY
ALLOWS *for Anne*

Boyer LEGEND Mouth

In me, muse,

As Helen Keller's

Teacher might, by

Nimble hand, somebody

Else's words: screen

Saver or duty

Roster, fleshed out

Skeleton key buried

Out of earshot
Of the living
Memory of X,

Y, Z, hand-
Made letters litter
The meaning, leaving

The song intact.
ONLY CURRENCY ENDURES
—And yet, erosion

Shapes the course,

Carrying price beyond

Reach. Watching, we

Endure the stench

Of the dead

Weight of profit

Wasting away. AMERICA

From bended knee

To wounded smile

In drag, plentiful
As the folds
Of a dress.

The surplus embryo
Of a nascent
Idea, frozen in

Time. CONGEALED LABOR
At the feet
Of a bank

Of a river
Of gold flowing
Vertically from ranks

Of clerical workers
To the managing
General partner up

Above, the edifice
Of money merely
Redirects the shine

Around a shadow
Of my former
Self. Light flows,

Leaving black ink
Behind, but never
Enough. COINAGE Intellect

Is a hard
Currency that jangles
Happily in pursed

Lips. ALIENATION Imprisoned

In a book

Used for pillow

By a head

Dreaming of things

Kept out of

Consciousness—an untrained

Nameless urge buried

In a windowed

Envelope. It must

Be methodical, must

Be a strict

Translation of sounds

Threading intimations through

An eye so

Narrow, light misses

The mark. WARTIME

ECONOMY For shame

Of a whimper
The dog kneeled.
His heart died

But its master
Lived on, liquefied,
And inexact, moving

And eroding organ
Transplanted from continent
To continent. WORKER

True to type,
The blind leading
The blind talk

To the hand
Because the face
Isn't listening. Assaulted

By quick frequencies
Of color, work
Is a poem

Learned by heart
And forgotten, contained
Like a meaning,

Yet containing none,
The deep end
Of a tight

Pocket, a password
Protected brain function
Written to disc.

Fifty: THE EMERGENCY
BROADCASTING SYSTEM What
Do you get

When you cross
A yellow peril
With a red

Menace? An orange
Alert. The sky
With a mind

Of its own
Dissipating matter drops
Cold rain, heavy

Snow, confronts earth
With a different
Temp. Let these

Predictable effects occur
Across a wider
Demographic. Nothing is

Forever: ink dries

Up, insight fades

Away, events require

Reconstruction, buildings require

Plans. Pull-down

Boxes, their discrete

Categories filling heads

Swimming a crawl

At the bottom

Of a screen,
Eyes averted, flatten
Under huge blocks

Of stone, where
People spend so
Much of their

Lives, loving nothing
But their own
Derangements: *we who*

Are the voice
Recognition software impairing
The response time

Essential for recovery
Of their black
Boxes hesitate. Click.

The missing inaction
Definitive of peace
Becomes malevolent, disdaining

The waves bringing
News of war
To our kingdom.

Fifty-one: THE
AUTHORITARIAN PERSONALITY He
Who spat out

Commands like mouthwash
Didn't deign to
Wash the sink-

Ing feeling of
Disdain away when
Done. **Fifty-two:**

WORRYING A LINE
Let the furnace
Glow with wounded

Pride, bells ring
With thickening tongue.
Let the breeze

Tease the leaves

Tearing themselves free

From the branch.

Take away substance

From shadow, let

The narrowest margin

Of material existence

Cover us in

Darkness. When lines

Are pulled taut,
The words spill
Free. Let them

Expire, like sighs
From a syllable.
Let the lines

Move slowly through
Every innocent conversation.
Let the lines

Move quickly through
Every guilty thought.
Let debris re-

Assemble our world,
The wind whistle
Hatikva. The difference

Between a sieve
And a civilization
Is the size

Of the hole,

Not the character

Of what it

Lets through. **Fifty-**
Three: SONNET FROM
THE BOURGEOISIE There

The form supersedes

The content, here

The content supersedes

The form: the
Piled illusions of
Democrats, reconciled in

Struggle—displaced by
Cudgels of fear.
A woman cries

"Gendarme! Gendarme!" in
Clear accents faithfully
Copied from a

Child. Hostile troglodytes,
Undefiled, reach out
To smash a

Face that held
Me dear. With
Feverish eyes, toppled

Statues heave the
Word that stone
Couldn't animate. Discharged

Soldiers prick a
Bubble: truth. Socialist
Castles in the

Air fall straight-
Way to the
Ground. North sweeps

Away the south,
Its class position
To annihilate. **Fifty-**

Four: PLEASE HELP
US IN TEXAS
Two years ago

My high school
Sophomore got on
An Ezra Pound

Listserv to get
Help on his
Research paper. We

Have tried following

The procedure exactly

At least 15

Times to get

Off. We've been

Nice. We've been

Mean. We've written

To the school

Numerous times. PLEASE

PLEASE get us
Off! My gosh,
The child is

Graduated now and
Not even home
And you still

Keep us on
The list. Poets
Are great, but

Quite frankly, we
HATE Ezra Pound.
Can you help?

Fifty-five: RED
INK The face
Of industry shows

No contrition, yet
Lets tears fall
Wastefully, knowing well

A tax base
Always arises to
Absorb the loss.

Fifty-six: SEQUELA
A quickly scribbled
Thought denting every

Subsequent record presses
Into the mind,
Which never evens:

Consciousness is wadded.
A book dropped
In water, expanding

Under the sun,
Is still readable,
Though its stiff

Warped pages turn
Awkwardly. **Fifty-seven:**
GRACE *for Dan,*

Kate, Anna, Maggie
Make it new
World, though old

Habits are what
Mostly grow there.
A final harvest

Of good intentions
Gone to seed.
In need, we

Read the Bible

For directions home,

But no one

Lives there anymore

And dinner's ready

Here. **Fifty-eight:**

REVOLUTIONARY PROGRAM *"The*

Answer very often

Is to add,

In the right
Place, the simple
Word 'not'"—Laura

Riding If the
Death of the
Author requires an

Execution of intention,
Then the ghost
Of meaning will

Assume the form

Of aimless scribble—

Or not. **Fifty-**

Nine: IN ADVANCE

OF A BROKEN

ARM Thought leans

Like a shovel

In a shed

Against familiar limits

Framing the cold

Truth of incessant

Labor. The night

Falling as softly

As snow, covering

Our consciousness of

Exhaustion. **Sixty:** CLICK

HERE *for Elaine*

Equi MORE STUFF

ABOUT BEN: I

Am an individual.

I love being

Me. I am

Outspoken, silly, emotional,

Sensitive, obsessive, extravagant,

Vulgar, loud and

Kind. I am

More than just

A pretty face!
NICKNAMES: Freeloader, Buzz,
Professor, Queen of

Cute, Green Eyes,
Beddu. DREAMS IN
LIFE: To speak

Italian, to sing
In tune, to
Move to Rome

With Carla and
Become a famous
Expatriate. To make

The world a
Better place. *I*
May not have

Zillions of buddies
But I do
Have good friends

I love dearly. You
Guys mean the
World to me,

Even if we
Never see each
Other any more.

WHAT I LOVE:
Rental cars, snow
Days, snuggling in

Bed, gel pens,

Flannel sheets, popcorn,

Soccer, the Internet,

'70s stuff (punk

Rock, disco, language

Poetry, the whole

Deal), my wife

Carla, my cat

Domenico, Teletubbies, slippers,

sixty

The I Ching,
Talking on the
Phone, sitting by

The sea with
A fat book,
Sunshine, butterflies, glitter,

"Star Trek Voyager,"
Deconstruction, cool hats,
My school, soul

Music...and loads
More! WHAT A
SURPRISE, MORE ABOUT

ME! *Fave celebs:*
Amiri Baraka, Nanni
Moretti, Delilah, Hannah

Ashrawi, the Olsen
Twins and Ty.
Pennington. *Fave foods:*

Pasta, sardines, Ben
& Jerry's "Chunkie
Monkey" ice cream,

Compari, pears, polenta,
Eggplant, and asparagus.
STUFF I HATE

WITH A PASSION!
Snobby people, annoying
Jingles, bugs (except

Ladybugs and butterflies),
Lacan, nasty people
Who can't mind

Their own damn
Business! spam mail,
Gooey price tags

On books, the
Sight of blood,
Religious freaks, being

Short on cash,
Rejection letters, bottled
Salad dressing, slow

Computers, crowded malls.
STUFF THAT WILL
ALWAYS BE COOL!

Italian food, summers
By the sea,
My wife, smileys,

For Better or
For Worse, secular
Humanism, sex, color

Plates in art
Books, E. E.
Cummings, road trips,

Shopping, licorice, candles,
Champagne, Italy, individuality,
Web pages like

This one...and

Me! **Sixty-one:**

ECOPOETICS STATEMENT Language

Is a dumping

Ground that produces

Its own contents.

Sixty-two: AGAINST

THE TIDE They

Deny the Holocaust,

But not the
Parting of the
Red Sea—which

Is how we
Entered history in
The first place.

After Auschwitz, all
Art is belligerent,
But not belligerent

Enough. **Sixty-three:**
PHENOMENOLOGIES *for Rod*
Smith FORGOTTEN UPON

WAKING Hilted memory
Takes a thrust
And pulls away

The hand, which
Then relaxes, dropping
The matter altogether.

DÉJÀ VU Sliding
Out of view,
Memory glimpses back

At us, like
An eye staring
Into a head

From which it
Fixes a view
In the other

Direction—impossibly. SELF-
RECRIMINATION It all
Makes so much

Sense, and hurts
Too clearly in
The wrong place:

A sewing needle
Drawn through its
Own eye, tightening

The logic. THERAPY
A curdled muscle
Drops a foot

In a clump
On the unfeeling
Floor. Sensate, voiceless,

Hard as wood,
Muddled as thought,
Scraped into consciousness

By a glacier
Of calcified will.
FRIDAY NIGHT All

Our language frazzled
To a cloud
Of intuition, whetted

On the lip
Of a rusty
Knife's blunt edge

Of an understanding
Tongue that cuts
Our loss. OPTIMISM

Draining the glass
Halved, then emptied
Of meaning, consciousness

Is unbecomingly drunk
On hope. VOICE
Sound constitutes this

World whose changes

Make song excite

Sense: memory, a

Spindle willing it

All around us

Again in slow

Revolution. IDENTITY Little

By little enough

Recompense for what

Suspends judgment eases

Memory: the self

Is a three-

Dimensional object without

Obverse, modeled from

Life. DIURNAL Powders

In a puddle

In a jar

Seep down, slowly,

Changing color as
We look out,
Seeing the light

Fall behind, giving
Way to dust
Hiding the sunset

Inside us. PARA-
PRAXIS A spoken
Word has no

Real direction, wriggling
Every which way
To escape capture.

In every head
A trap, a
Rat tail torn

Away in a
Bloody mouth. REASON
Walking on egg-

Shell like ridges
Of hardened slush,
The active mind

Feels heavy, crushing
The very thought
Supporting its progress.

Sixty-four: THE
DEFENSE OF MARRIAGE
ACT The urge,

The indestructible urge

To combine incomes

In a family

Way, to put

One's affairs in

A long-term

Care option. Love

Is a bed-

Time story that

Did its trick.

Marriage, a bar-

Coded product whose

Replacement parts must

Be scavenged from

Junkyards. **Sixty-five:**

FIN DE SIECLE

For services rendered

By thought balloon—

Punctured hopes return
To sender; familiarity
Bleeds consent, biting

A tongue off
The record in
Hunger for silence.

A bigger slice
Of the pie
In the sky

Is falling down
And leaking through
Shuttered windows, fluttering

Hearts, golden arches
Along our death
March. Like flies

On shit, America,
Your God abhors
A vacuum cleaner.

Go fuck your
Anatomically correct dollar
Bill. This is

Not a pipe
Bomb, though it
Explodes: the difference

Between prince charming
And horny toad.
Sixty-six: ICE

CUBE TRAY *for*
Kit Robinson Opaque
Enough to hold

Thought afloat upon
Its own more
Liquid substance, language

Freezes memory into
Grids of words
Ready for use.

Sixty-seven: PETRARCHAN
SONNET A b
B a a

B b a
C d c
D c d.

Sixty-eight: TONGUE
DEPRESSOR Magnetically ugly
Pig that fails

To make hay
Bail water from
A drunken boat-

Swain's whistler's mother-
Fucking ball hog
Going wild rice

For Roni-sized
Madidi, Bolivia's spectacular
New national park.

Sixty-nine: AGAINST
AUTOMATIC WRITING My
Rude awakening disdains

To please compliant
Metaphors requesting release.
From what? From

Dreams that money
Can't buy fast
Enough to saturate

Demand: a mattress

Wet from lack

Of self-control.

Seventy: STUPIDAGGINI *"Jumbled*

In one common /

Box / Of their

Dark stupidity, / Orchid,

Swan, and Caesar

Lie"—W. H.

Auden NONSENSE SONG

Let no man

Tear asunder flower

From stem, nor

Them who understand

And care wear

Out their blunder

In their hair.

Bare need gone

To seed still

Celebrates May when

Only Must remains.

PAY ATTENTION Prosody

Counts for nothing

And free verse

Isn't free; allusion

Is the product

Placement of poetry.

OPACITY I can't

See the forest

For the falling

Trees making noteworthy

Noise, but only

Poetry's noise can

Stay news, and

Only when readers

Consent to be

Confused. ENNUI Undulating
Smoke rings rolling
Open like some

Muscular spasm. Their
Ohs we can't
Fathom: crepuscular poetry

Formed by lips
Bored by words
And their relationships.

APPARITION Desire recedes

Like a hairline,

Revealing naked power—

An overweight gent

About fifty-five

With a hardon

In the shower.

THE GORDIAN POEM

To snarl a

String and spend
One's whole wrong
Life unraveling its

Knot, is only
Just the beginning
Of getting what

Alexander forgot: fates
Are loosened, not
Divined, while swords

That cut the
Strongest twine, fret
The future of

A line. GRIEF
Tears don't come
From the eyes,

But someplace farther
Back, where light
Can't penetrate. Pools

Of standing water
Behind the mind
Collect, occasionally rise

To overflow. BLURB
The lyric is
A poem containing

Hysterical symptoms. Expressions
Of defeat disguised
As jests, these

Poems light a

Flaming dessert bulimics

Eat for want

Of sense, and

Can't throw up,

And won't digest.

HACK WORK There

Once was a

Bishop from Rwanda,

Who raised his
Benedictions with a
Din, flexed by

Muscles in a
Phantom limerick torn
From hymn to

Hymn. THE AROMA
Stung by the
Memory of a

Bee who made

Love to a

Flower and moved

On. SERMON When

The final day

Comes we will

Give no quarter

But a dollar

To the beggar,

And the suitcase

Will lie down

With the porter.

HISTORICAL ANECDOTE Cleo

Said, "Stay clear

Of hungry men

Who stare, at

Inspiration pushing through

The pipeline of

Despair." "A mistress
With her hand
Held out, reaching

For a ring,"
Said Caesar, "Cuts
Loose now and

Then a puppet
From the string."
Seventy-one: MY

CALLING Forensic doctor
Of philosophy, greeting-
Card carrying member

Of the sickly
Bourgeoisie—that's me.
But don't worry,

If I speak
Loftily when defending
A prejudice, that's

Just the voice

Of universal history

Sounding out the

Limits of the

Text. **Seventy-two:**

ZIONISM There are

Times to talk,

And times to

Fill your mouth

With sand. There
Is a road
Map, but the

Roads have been
Erased. There is
An accord, but

The parties have
Been killed. Ants
Ordered by ants

Build their colony
Underground. Trash blown
Aloft, like a

Child's heaven raised
Upon cloud. Worm's
Meat: retreat into

Dust. Dust: rise
Up, vanquish our
View. View: surrender

Your colors to
The night. Night:
Settle like dust

In our mouths.
Seventy-three: AFTER
LEVINAS *for Jill*

Robbins Philosophy is
A pencil sharpened
At both ends,

Blunting the point,
Writing two soliloquies
At once. **Seventy-**

Four: "THERE ARE
THINGS / WE LIVE
AMONG 'AND TO

SEE THEM / IS
TO KNOW OURSELVES'"
When sight becomes

Mechanical, hidden objects
Come to light,
Darken recognition. Lifted

By a claw
From among furred
Animals, the object

Of desire rewards
The avaricious patience
Of a child.

Seventy-five: JAWS
OF LIFE Language
Is a tool

For extricating the
Mind from an
Accident of the

Mind's own devising.
Seventy-six: RENDER
UNTO CAESAR Profiles

On a coin
Record divinity's weight
In gold. Mere

Ghosts of exchange
Value, they offer
No resistance, giving

No ground either.
Listen: the rootless
Wind is stirring

Up the trees,
Leaving us in
Awe outside their

Circle. **Seventy-seven:**
EPIPHANY The metaphor
Of speech creates

Meaning without vocality—
But even noise
Becomes articulate when

Described. The flapping
Tape, the gurgling
Pipes, are sounds

That speak of
The structure of
Our lives. Objects

Near at hand
Are no more
Credible than those

In mind. Rhetoric,

Not faith, presents

The evidence of

Things unseen. **Seventy-**

Eight: PATER NOSTER

A coveted mirage

Dispelled by grief

Sustains belief: our

Father, he is

The very air
We breathe. We,
The living, see

By his light;
The dead cannot
Escape his notice.

Worm your way
Into a heart-
Hardened thought's infirm

Grounding, the caws

Of an ill

Effect will still

Be heard above

You. **Seventy-nine:**

ALETHEIA Truly I

Can think truth

Only as a

Sink, down whose

Drain all clarity
Streams, to keep
The filthy clean.

Eighty: PARADISE Using
The same shaded
Meanings a tree

Fails to raise
In anger against
The sun, creation

Becomes an argument

Against the God

Who established its

Limits. For all

That is, is

Because it cannot

Trespass upon nothing,

Ignorance of which

Was bliss, once

Upon a time.
Painful, to fall
Silent at brink

Of knowledge, learn
Nothing and lose
Hope: a rope

Burns our hands
When we slide
Away from its

Knitted telos. **Eighty-**
One: SICILY *for*
Laura Billitteri THE

NEW GOSPEL Television
Is a shepherd
Who breaks your

Wall to feed
His sheep. LIBRINO
These humble shoes

Are a relic
Making a cathedral
Of the world.

PANE COTTO A
Hard life, softened
In the milk

Of human kindness,
Makes a simple
Fare, perhaps the

Best. JUSTICE Resting
On his three
Wheels, the old

Man weighs my
Ability to pay
In a scale

Without numbers. BLACK
SMOKE The Etna
Is still undecided.

RADIO MARIA A

Swaying bridge attached

To no bank

Supports the weight

Of a single

Pedestrian thought. CARTOLINE

ILLUSTRATE *Rovine* The

Roman stones remain

Where the new

Bricks crumble. *Vicino*

A Enna A

Brick house cracked

At the center

Like a fossilized

Egg. *Banco di*

Nuvole A hole

In the sky

Where the silver

Leaks away illuminates
The fields. *Centro
Storico* An old,

Familiar face, stripped
Of its smile,
Peeled from tomorrow's

Election. BOURGEOIS INTERIOR
Ornately framed in
Silver that shines

From perpetual service,
Tarnished souls look
Back at themselves,

All business. LA
ROTATORIA You can
Bully your way

In, or ease
In gently, if
You belong. PUPPET

THEATER One scene
Turns into another,
Like the generations

Of a family
Of thieves that
Relieves you of

Your burden. Pulling
The strings necessary
To make something

Happen, the bodies
Pile and you
Can't help but

Smile when it's
Over. MAFIA Blown
Out of proportion

Like all judgment
That fails, finality
Is a means

To an end.
PIAZZA VITTIME DEL
DOVERE Time hollows

Out the solidity
Of our world,
Leaving us standing

On the corpses
Of ghosts of
Heroes, eating sweets.

PUBLIC MENACE Sleepless

Dogs lie through

Their teeth at

Us—and we

Let them. THE

ELEPHANT, CATANIA Our

Outsized self-image,

Installed in public,

Atop a pedestal,

Self-reliant. Never
Native to these
Shores, but formed

From our lava:
The soul of
Servitude, defiant. ARITHMETIC

To multiply fractions
Requires the permission
Of a number

Of important persons.
VIEW OF THE
CITY Rules were

Made to be
Broken like a
Nose: it heals,

But never looks
The same. Palermo,
Your face has

Character, but when
You smile your
Eyes show some-

Thing else. UN
AMARO When something
Sticks in your

Throat and getting
Angry will only
Make it worse,

There's this: bitterness.
PORTO PALO Here
Where the waters

Meet, the indolent
Come to show
That their split

Natures also lap
The edges of
A dream. Sicily,

When sun elongates

Shadows till they

Cover all the

Earth, we put

Our currents in

Your current by

The sea. **Eighty-**

Two: STILL LIFE

The inner workings

Of a locked
Suitcase studied on
Screen. **Eighty-three:**

OUT LIKE A
LAMB I love
This last moment

Of bareness before
Spring, when trees
Brush the air

Delicately, with filaments
Of wood. Under
A weak sun,

Unwanted hills slip
Away, leaving cold
Ground softening brownly,

Yielding to a
Human weight. **Eighty-
Four:** THE VISIBLE

WORD *for Johanna*
Drucker **I** was
A stuck key

In Berkeley, California,
And every time
The **QUICK BROWN**

FOX tried jumping
Over the **LAZY**
DOG, I held

Him fast between

The "**U**" and

The "**C**"—till

He cried mercy,

Or chewed off

His serif getting

Free. **Eighty-five**:

REVOLUTIONARY PATIENCE *For*

Askia Touré Some

Love to sail

Or swim, I

Love the ocean

For its power

To erode. Hope

Is an ocean

Of feeling, strong

As the current

Pulling me along

These rocks. **Eighty-
Six:** DEVOTIONAL IMAGE
The bus kneeling

Down to your
Wheelchair. **Eighty-seven:**
POETRY AND POLITICS

For Hannah Arendt
History's loyal opposition,
The Imagination, settles

A claim you

Reject on principle.

Now flowers doom

The sun to

A life of

Dying color. O

Let the arrogance

Of our rage

Blot the page

Whenever we cry
Over spilled milk
And honeyed lies.

Incurring a debt
Then letting it
Slide, through the

Checkpoints of un-
Guarded thought, in
Palestine. **Eighty-eight:**

HUMANISM Write blood
In dust, write
Words in marble,

Though all blood
Is alike ancient,
And all carved

Sentiments cast in-
Substantial shadows. **Eighty-
Nine:** KEYSTROKE REGIME

Let prose solicitation
Fill the tape,
And let all

Messages be collect,
If every line
Must be on

Tap, and every
Word we speak
Suspect. To drag

And click work-
Product into trash
Cans then empty

The been-there-
And-done-that-
There fool has

Dragged us in
To a work-
Product related disaster

Coverage. Bullet-proof,
Written in steel,
Then polished off

In a meal.
Buried in sand
Falling through glass

Perpetually turned over
In its grave
Element, democracy: who

Can say what
Baffles protect us
From, per hour?

Ninety: PERVERSION Take
A deep swallow
Of pride coming

Before a fall,
Then brace yourself
For a landing.

Compelling feelings repel
The imagination, which
Still submits, warily.

Normality is one
Extreme among others.
Ninety-one: NURSERY

RHYME Rock smashes
Scissors that cut
The paper that

Employs the words

That relinquish control

Of hands throwing

Stones at a

Couple of scholars

Armed with machine-

Guns while out

On patrol. **Ninety-**

Two: BREATH UNIT

The bell clerk's
Tears for Fears
Album kept playing

On my nerves
Of steel-belted
Radials blown out

On the road
To another lonely
One-night stand.

Ninety-three: YEOMAN'S

SERVICE I'd like

To put my

Foot in it,

Or yours, testing

The bottom since

It can't be

Seen: holes filled

With applicants dully

Formed out of
Clay. Contingents, contingencies,
En route, enraged,

Swallow whole, re-
Gurgitate, the biomass
Of Christendom: what

Does not change
Is the will
To power; Daniel

In the lion's
Den had the
Most advanced radar

System in creation.
Ninety-four: STATEMENT
OF PRINCIPLE *for*

Benjamin Hollander We
Who experience history
As an inter-

Generational effect develop
Symptoms of other
People's memories, then

Fend off an
Embarrassment of riches
Of distress. For

Less is always
More of the
Same old shit:

Knowledge for which

One has no

Words, only self-

Destructive actions that

Feel good, but

Bear no future

Scrutiny. **Ninety-five:**

THE NEW COLOSSUS

Can you get

Up the flag
On the pole
Of your warbling

Hope's loyalty? Red
Letters date us
By the page

We scrape by
On, the whale
Of a lie

That swallowed up
The profit motive.
Give us your

Tired laws, your
Poor excuse of
A national anthem,

Your Hungry Man
TV dinners. Though
Yearning to be

Free of debt,

Our filched cigarettes

Detest the flame,

Circling the brain

Drain we call

America. **Ninety-six:**

SOCIAL ENGINEERING Stored

In a nut-

Shell of male

Need. A needle-
Nosed-pliers-like
Bird's bill opens:

I withdraw expensive
Seed. An activity
Goes on, determined

By an impulse
To deny mothering
To a worm-

Like appendage with
Plumage, theorized from
Available facts. Here,

Where decay means
Fertility and breeds
Life, the diagnostician

Of magical forbearance
Whets the appetite
Of a knife,

But means well.

Ninety-seven: SEVEN

DAYS IN ANOTHER

COUNTRY *for Salvo*

Marano DOMENICA Eye

For an eyesore,

Tooth for a

Toothache. The neon

Cross turned off

In the public
Square, where even
Pigeons are on

The take. LUNEDÍ
Qualunquista, you wear
Gene Hackman's grimace

Staring *Under Suspicion*
From every other
Plastered wall's pink

Face, showing nary

A trace of

Blemish, you are

Yourself a blemish.

MARTEDÍ All roads

Lead beyond Rome

To northern banks,

Where southern rivers

Of gold erode

All confidence, leaving

The dirt intact

For a drive

Back home. MERCOLEDÍ

Schiavó: Enslaved (also

A place name).

Malerba: Bad Seed

(Another place). Unruly

Flowers follow along

As we follow

The sea. Golden

Switchbacks overhead lead

Into creeping green.

GIOVEDÍ Blame narrow

Streets for minds

Entwined in tit-

For-tat's chit-

Chat gratification, then

Cobble together a
Few stoned winks
And deliver our

Drinks, dear waiter.
It's later than
You think. VENERDÍ

A sardine can
With grinding gears
Drips oil. Cats

Hide underneath. Pokemon

Balloons blow free

From a jitney

On a string.

I can't understand

Anything. Let's eat.

SABATO A dumptruck

Loaded with rocks

And gravel slows

Traffic for hours

Along decimated orange

Groves (where Myrmidons

Pump gas for

Egypt), inspiring yet

Again the extra-

Parliamentary left turn

Over traffic islands

To Mount Etna's

Chinese beard. Empty-
Headed sky. **Ninety-
Eight:** SELF-PRESERVATION

Buffered by dreams:
The mind is
Like the cotton

In an aspirin
Bottle, absorbing moisture,
Keeping the bitter

Pills from breaking
Down. **Ninety-nine**:
NETWORK NEWS Bursts

Of attention set
End to end
Tire the mind,

Which then relaxes.
Like a cat
Who has never

Known the open
Air, but sees
The world through

A window frame,
We sleepily watch
Our unattainable prey.

One Hundred: NINE
RIDDLES *for the*
Daughters of memory

ONE I am

Standing water, rain

Driving over shadows

Of green trees

By degrees. Massing

On the borders

Of an immature

Thought, I am

The questioning glance

Of a blow
To the head,
A neglected utterance

Extending sympathy beyond
Hope. What am
I? TWO My

Feet are firmly
On the ground
Crumbling underfoot. I

Change my mind
The way an
Ocean changes color,

Giving little glimmers
Of what's under.
A machine without

Replacement parts, a
Urine-rusted radiator
Can express me.

THREE Do you
Know me? I
Am the darkening

Of light, a
Breathless victim rising
From the bottom

Of a pool
Of sweat. Slippery
When all wet,

Tanned from artificial

Light, my world

Is an iron

Filing pulled by

A magnetized tear.

FOUR I am

Sysadmin, a domain

Name, table crumbs

And the bugs

Who eat them.

I am pierced

Ears strung by

Pearls, the sloping

Roof who dropped

The ball. I

Am newfangled things

—Bloatware, chick cars—

And all things

That are old.

I am German

Chancellor Gerhard Schroeder's

Brother Lothar, cleaning

Sewers after four

Years on welfare.

Is there anything

I cannot include?

You tell me.

FIVE The shadowy

Corner that resists

A wide broom

Without whom no

Conscience is clean

Contains me utterly

On all sides.

But *I* contain

All sides. Guess

Who. SIX Do

Not rebuke me.

I was born

Against the grain

Of a cross

Word made flesh,

Dishonoring my parents

With every drawn

Breath. Oops, I

Did it again.
SEVEN Lengthening waves
Of A.M.

Radio penetrate my
Thought. Can you?
EIGHT A flip

Book that scatters
Images and innuendos.
A drainage ditch

Clogging the eye-
Sore next door
With the sound

Of drinking games.
Name my tune,
I am yours.

NINE The needle
Snaps but my
Thread still holds

one hundred

A button to

The hole. Me:

A loose string

Of words whose

Only purpose was

To keep a

Light-hearted moment

From slipping away.

What am I?

Numerical Index
(with page numbers)

ALPHABETICAL INDEX
(with etude and page numbers)

ACKNOWLEDGMENTS

Some of these etudes first appeared as Backwoods Broadside no. 59 (published by Sylvester Pollet), and in the following books, pamphlets, and journals: *The Baffler* (Jennifer Moxley, poetry ed.); *Can I Have My Ball Back* (Jim Behrle, ed.); *Ecopoetics* (Jonathan Skinner, ed.); *The Gig* (Nate Dorward, ed.); *The Hat* (Jordan Davies, ed.); *In Your Ear Postcard Series* (Jules Boykoff, ed.); *Jacket* (John Tranter, ed.); *Kenning* (Patrick Durgin, ed.); *One Hundred Days: An Anthology*, ed. Andrea Brady (Cambridge: Barque Press, 2001); *Quid* (Keston Sutherland, ed.); *Readme* (Gary Sullivan, ed.); *Shofar* (Daniel Morris, guest ed.); *Situation* (Mark Wallace, ed.); *Stolen Island Review* (John Hyland and Michael Roberson, eds.); and *The Best American Poetry 2002*, ed. Robert Creeley (New York: Scribners, 2002). Joyce Susskind set the first etude to music; the song was subsequently performed by Nancy Ogle and Ginger Hwalek; Giovanni Miraglia produced an Italian version of the eighty-first. Other poems first circulated or appeared on the following websites as text- or soundfiles: *Equanimity* (Jordan Davies' blog), *PennSound*, and *Unprotected Texts* (Tom Beckett's blog). Kenneth Irby's *Études* long ago planted a thought—he is but one of many interlocutors not named in these studies. My thanks as well to Kyle Schlesinger, for realizing this poem in three dimensions; and Rod Smith for giving it a fourth.   —B.F.

edge books

CROW Rod Smith, Leslie Bumstead, eds. $6
CUSPS Chris Stroffolino $3
FELONIES OF ILLUSION Mark Wallace $15
HAZE: ESSAYS POEMS PROSE Mark Wallace $14
NOTHING HAPPENED AND BESIDES I WASN'T THERE
    Mark Wallace $9.50

a e r i a l   m a g a z i n e
(edited by Rod Smith)

Aerial 10: LYN HEJINIAN co-edited by Jen Hofer forthcoming 2012 $20
Aerial 9: BRUCE ANDREWS $15
Aerial 8: BARRETT WATTEN $35
Aerial 6/7: featuring JOHN CAGE $25

Literature published by Aerial/Edge is available through:

Small Press Distribution
www.spdbooks.org
1-800-869-7553
orders@spdbooks.org

or

Edge Books
PO Box 25642
Georgetown Station
Washington, DC 20027

When ordering from Aerial/Edge directly, add $1 postage for
individual titles. Two or more titles postpaid. For more
information please visit our website at www.aerialedge.com.